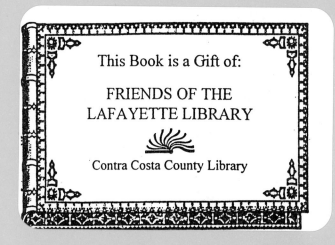

ESSENTIAL
Arts and Crafts

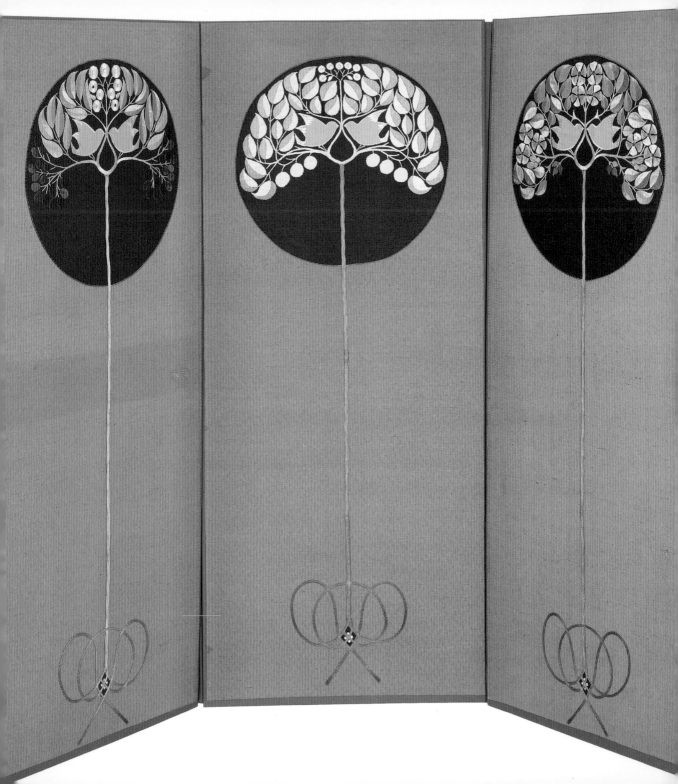

ESSENTIAL
Arts and Crafts

Karen Livingstone

V&A Publications

First published by V&A Publications, 2005
V&A Publications
160 Brompton Road
London SW3 1HW

Distributed in North America by Harry N. Abrams, Inc., New York

ISBN 1 85177 447 5

Library of Congress Control Number 2004111388

A catalogue record for this book is available from the British Library.

Designed by Broadbase

All new V&A photography by Christine Smith of the V&A Photographic Studio

Front jacket illustration: Charles Rennie Mackintosh, hall chair. Oak, stained dark with rush seat. Britain, 1901. For Windyhill, Kilmacolm. © Hunterian Museum and Art Gallery, University of Glasgow Mackintosh Collection.

Back jacket illustration: Hamada Shōji, dish (see plate 80).

Frontispiece: M.H. Baillie Scott, panels for a screen. Silk appliqué on a cotton and hemp ground (mounted on new support). Britain, c.1896. Embroidered by Mrs Baillie Scott. V&A:T.127-1953

Contents page: C.F.A. Voysey, desk. Oak with brass panel and copper hinges. Britain, 1896. Metalwork by W.B. Reynolds. For Mr and Mrs Ward-Higgs. V&A:W.6-1953

Printed in China

V&A Publications
160 Brompton Road
London SW3 1HW
www.vam.ac.uk

CONTENTS

1
C.F.A. Voysey, clock. Mahogany, painted and gilded, brass and steel. Britain, 1895–6. Case made by Frederick Coote. Movement made by Camerer, Cuss and Co.
V&A: W.5-1998

INTRODUCTION

Arts and Crafts was one of the most far-reaching and influential international design movements of modern times. It was the first major art movement to focus on the decorative arts, and the first to be directed at the reform of art at every level and across a broad social spectrum, from ordinary worker to aristocratic patron, simple country cottage to city mansion. Based on new ideas about work, life and the home, and drawing on the pioneering spirits of reform and enterprise, the Arts and Crafts Movement spread across Britain, Europe, America and Japan, and sometimes even further afield, changing the way we think about design for the home and how we value the way things are made. The movement, which first emerged in its fullest form in Britain in the 1880s, grew out of an increasing concern about the effects of industrial manufacture on standards of design, and the debilitating impact of industrialization on social conditions and traditional craftsmanship. It challenged the traditional hierarchies in the arts, campaigning to raise the status of the craftsman and designer, and aiming to 'turn our artists into craftsmen and our craftsmen into artists'.[1] Inspired by the pioneers and founders of the movement in Britain, including William Morris, Walter Crane and C.R. Ashbee, a set of idealistic principles for living and working were developed through

the Arts and Crafts Movement. These included the revival of traditional handicrafts and techniques, a return to a simpler way of life, and an improvement in daily existence through the design, manufacture and use of domestic items – or, in the words of one of the pioneers of the movement, finding 'beauty in everyday things' and encouraging the 'making [of] beautiful things for the homes of simple and gentle folk'.[2]

It flourished in Britain, America and Europe from the 1880s to *c*.1916, and in Japan from 1926 to 1945. Across this wide geographic spread, the Arts and Crafts Movement was bound by a unity of ideas and a common purpose to establish a new democratic ethic for living and working in the modern world. In each country specific social, political, regional and national needs influenced the type of work that was produced. Although Arts and Crafts was primarily driven by the ideas and philosophies set out by its leaders, there was, nonetheless, an identifiable set of design characteristics that is associated with the movement and naturally emerged from the principles that underpinned it. Reflecting a balance between technique and design and the principle of collaboration between designer and craftsman, who should work together 'hand in hand, and work *head* with hand',[3] the architecture and objects of the Arts and

2
William Morris, John Henry
Dearle and Philip Webb, *The
Forest*, tapestry. Woven silk and
wool. Britain, 1887. Made by
Morris & Co.
V&A:T.111-1926

Crafts Movement drew on both tradition and innovation, combining the revival of styles and techniques with a new approach to design and decoration. They include both simple and highly decorative examples, and manifest a sympathetic and appropriate use of materials and techniques as well as a love of nature and the vernacular (PLATE 1).

William Morris and John Ruskin were two of the most important thinkers to influence the development of the Arts and Crafts Movement in Britain and internationally through their writings, which were widely

known and translated into many languages. By the 1880s Morris was a commercially successful designer and manufacturer, whose call for a radical shift in manufacturing processes was taken up by the Arts and Crafts Movement. The value he placed on work, practical skills and the joy of craftsmanship, and his appreciation of the natural beauty of materials, had led him to learn and revive earlier techniques and methods of manufacture such as natural dyeing, hand-block printing and tapestry weaving (PLATE 2). Ruskin's writings, particularly his chapter on 'The Nature of Gothic' in the second volume of *The Stones of Venice* (1853), and his views on the relationship between art and labour and on the moral significance of freedom of individual expression, were of enormous influence on the development of the movement.

Likewise, the process of design reform, which had been explored in Britain since the 1840s, and the new approach to the decorative arts by the architects of the Gothic Revival, including A.W.N. Pugin and Richard Norman Shaw, were important

antecedents to the movement. Indeed, many of the figures who were most influential in establishing the Arts and Crafts Movement in Britain, and its associated organizations such as the Art Workers Guild, founded in London in 1884, were architects.

Through the establishment of artistic guilds and exhibition societies, the publication of journals and magazines, and the exchange of ideas through meetings, travel, collecting and study, the Arts and Crafts Movement gathered pace from the 1890s and its ideals and philosophies spread and were widely adopted. Central to the ideals of the movement was a concern about the diminishing role of the craftsman as a result of the effects of increasing levels of industrial manufacture, which had effected a much commented-on serious decline in the social conditions and welfare of working people. The guilds and societies of the movement aimed to elevate the status of the craftsman and the individual through improved working conditions and by providing a forum for exhibitions and displays. This would also help elevate the status of the applied arts as a whole and through that demonstrate a conscious improvement in the application of art to everyday life.

While the importance of handicraft and traditional workshop production was clearly fundamental to the principles of the movement, there was also a very clear

3 OPPOSITE
Kate Bunce, *The Keepsake*.
Tempera on canvas. Britain,
1898–1901.
Birmingham Museum and Art Gallery

4 BELOW
Alexander Fisher, 'Peacock'
sconce. Steel, bronze, brass and
silver with enamelled
decoration. Britain, c.1899.
V&A: M.24-1970

5 OPPOSITE
Frank Lloyd Wright, 'Tree of
Life', window. Clear and iridized
glass, cathedral and gilded glass,
brass cames. America, c.1904.
One of 362 windows for the
Darwin Martin complex,
Buffalo, New York.
Martin House Restoration
Corporation

6 BELOW
Gustav Stickley, armchair. Oak,
leather. America, 1901. Made by
the Craftsman Workshops,
Syracuse, New York.
Private collection

intention within the Arts and Crafts
Movement to bring its influence to bear on
industrial design and manufacture, to
exchange and interact with the commercial
world, and to try to raise standards in
industrial design through example. In Britain
this was particularly evident in the
exhibitions of the Arts and Crafts Exhibition
Society, founded in 1887, and in the work of
architects and designers who forged links
with commercial manufacturers and retailers.
Through them, the Arts and Crafts style
became much more widely disseminated and
available to a wider consumer base, leading
one trade journal to comment:

> The arts and crafts movement has been
> the best influence on machine industry in
> the last ten years … while we have sought
> to develop handicraft beside it on sound
> and independent lines, we have succeeded
> in imparting something of the spirit
> of craftsmanship to the best kind of
> machine-work.[4]

In both America and the more industrialized
European countries, particularly Germany,
it was thought both relevant and appropriate
to use technology as a means of achieving
good quality design, efficiently produced
and available to a wider market, because it
was, inevitably, cheaper than individually
crafted items.

To a large extent the Arts and Crafts
Movement was an urban phenomenon,
driven by the forces and mechanisms of the

city, which provided the support network of art schools, exhibitions, societies and meeting places, as well as important access to sophisticated, educated and wealthy urban consumers. Prosperous cities such as London, Glasgow, Vienna, Budapest, Helsinki, Chicago or Tokyo provided the infrastructure and patronage that allowed the Arts and Crafts Movement to grow.

Alongside this, however, there was an increasing nostalgia for the countryside and vernacular traditions, which became, for many, central to the meaning of the movement. Nostalgic views of the countryside and rural traditions and practices were captured in the literature, music and images of the period (PLATE 8). For some, moving to the countryside to establish a new life and pursue traditional workshop practice was the fullest expression of the Arts and Crafts ideal and the simple life that they aspired to. Philanthropic efforts helped establish classes and workshops in rural areas, and these received support and exposure from the exhibitions and organizations of the movement. However, among the workshops and communities founded on Arts and Crafts principles, whether in Britain, Germany, Russia, Japan or elsewhere, the balance of power still remained with the educated and socially aware upper- and middle-class patrons and founders of these enterprises.

Nonetheless, the Arts and Crafts Movement in Britain can clearly be demonstrated to

7 OPPOSITE
Joseph Maria Olbrich, cabinet.
Maple wood inlaid with various
exotic woods. Germany, 1900.
Made by Hofmöbelfabrik Julius
Glückert, Darmstadt.
Museum Künstlerkolonie, Darmstadt

8 ABOVE
Peter Henry Emerson, *In the
Barley Harvest*. Photogravure
from *Pictures of East Anglian Life*,
London, 1888.
V&A: 51.C.36

9 ABOVE
Josef Hoffmann, brooch.
Silver, gold, moonstone,
amethyst, lapis lazuli, opal,
coral, agate, hematite, jasper,
tourmaline and other
semi-precious stones.
Austria, designed in 1908,
made in 1910. Made by
Eugen Pflaumer of the
Wiener Werkstätte.
Asenbaum Collection

10 OPPOSITE
Gerhard Munthe, *The
Daughters of the Northern
Lights (Aurora Borealis)* or
The Three Suitors, tapestry.
Linen and wool. Norway,
1896. Woven by Augusta
Christiansen at the
Nordenfjedske
Kunstindustrimuseum
Tapestry Studio, Trondheim.
Museum für Kunst und Gewerbe
Hamburg

have provided a model for workshop production, and to have encouraged the development of the individual. It also supported and encouraged the revival and development of a number of crafts and techniques including jewellery, textiles, furniture, ceramics, lettering and calligraphy, sgraffito, gesso, mural decoration, tempera painting (PLATE 3) and enamelling (PLATE 4). In America, bolstered by the much greater commercial awareness of a relatively young nation in the process of defining a national style and identity, architects, designers and entrepreneurs supplied furnishings both modest and sophisticated (PLATES 5, 6). A range of differing attitudes prevailed across Europe, dependent on existing workshop or industrial traditions, patronage and political identity, and rural or urban location. In Germany the relationship between art, craft and industry was most fully explored, and local manufacturing traditions were revived and supported by Arts and Crafts designers (PLATE 7). In Austria, which held a prosperous and politically stable position in the Central European region with a strong tradition in Vienna of high quality craftsmanship, the Arts and Crafts Movement centred around a new intellectual and avant-garde elite (PLATE 9). In Scandinavia the re-evaluation of traditional forms, subject matter and techniques provided the vehicle for the expression of a new national identity (PLATE 10). Finally, in Japan, a rediscovery of the

11 LEFT
Tomimoto Kenkichi,
octagonal lidded jar. White
porcelain. Japan, 1932.
National Museum of Modern
Art, Tokyo

12 OPPOSITE
Jar. White porcelain. Korea,
17th–18th century. Bought
in Seoul by Bernard Leach.
British Museum

vernacular, whether indigenous or exotic, provided a basis for the collecting and appreciation of traditional crafts, which in turn inspired new work by the artist-craftsmen of the Mingei movement (PLATES 11,12).

Common to all the countries in which the movement flourished was the enormous impact of Arts and Crafts ideals on domestic lifestyles and design for the home. William Morris's early example, at Red House in Bexleyheath, Kent, in the 1860s, aimed to create a way of living that was community-based, but also introduced art into every aspect of life, including functional domestic objects. From this time the home became the focal point in which the ideas and ideals of the Arts and Crafts Movement could be explored and expressed. Designed interiors, model rooms and even whole buildings became important ways of presenting (at international exhibitions, and in journals and publications) the Arts and Crafts concept that a home could be a total work of art, or *Gesamtkunstwerk*. Nothing in the domestic interior was too small or insignificant to be lovingly designed and made, and all were made to be seen and used together. The variety and range of manufacturing methods, and the varying levels of patronage in the Arts and Crafts Movement ensured that the Arts and Crafts home was explored at every level from the simplest cottage to the architect's grand vision, which could be realized only by the wealthiest clients,

and then very rarely in Britain.

Through the architects, designers and patrons of the Arts and Crafts Movement a new approach to design in the home as part of a complete way of life was established. The home became the focus of a moral, aesthetic and practical statement about how to live, and was the subject of many articles and discussions by the leading architects and designers of the movement. Indeed, in every aspect the Arts and Crafts Movement had an impact on design and the home, which continues to be reflected in the way we live and work today.

13
Lewis F. Day, cabinet. Oak, ebony
and satinwood inlays. Britain,
c.1888. Inlaid panels with signs
of the Zodiac executed by
George McCulloch. Shown
at the first exhibition of the
Arts and Crafts Exhibition
Society, 1888.
V&A: Circ.349-1955

BRITAIN

The Arts and Crafts Movement

The Arts and Crafts Movement took its name
from one of the first organizations formed to
unite and promote the work of like-minded
artists, designers and manufacturers, the
Arts and Crafts Exhibition Society. Through
its exhibitions in London from 1888 the
society aimed to raise the status of the
decorative arts, achieve recognition for the
individual maker, encourage the revival of
handicraft and influence an improvement
in industrial production (PLATE 13). The Arts
and Crafts Movement encouraged the unity
of all the arts, and included painters and
sculptors within its membership. The artist
John Duncan was just one of several painters
who combined the decorative technique of
tempera with subject matter drawn from
Celtic sources or historic myths and
legends (PLATE 14).

Arts and Crafts objects were made in a
wide variety of circumstances and using a
range of manufacturing techniques. For
example, William De Morgan ran a pottery in
London where ceramic blanks were decorated
with technically difficult, patterned lustre
glazes according to his designs and strict
instructions (PLATE 15). The metalworker
W.A.S. Benson, one of the founders of the
Arts and Crafts Exhibition Society, designed
pioneering electric light fittings and other

14
John Duncan, *St Bride*. Tempera
on canvas. Britain, 1913.
The National Gallery of Scotland

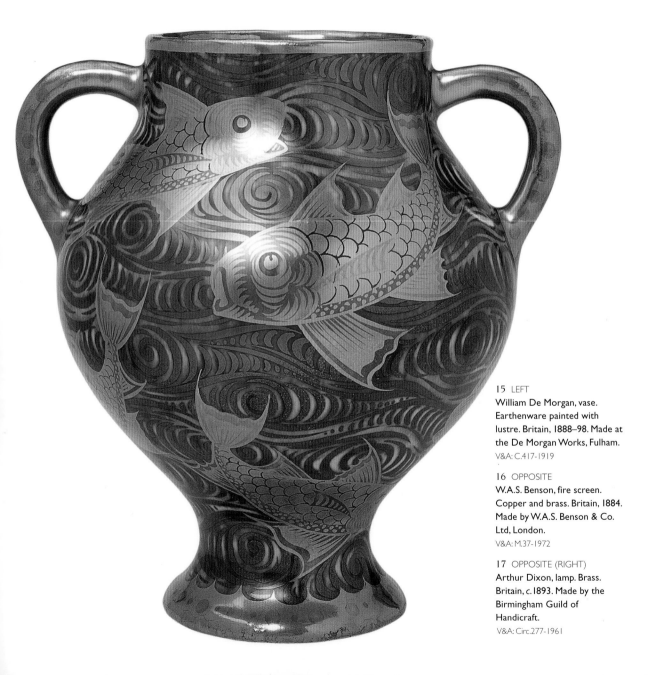

15 LEFT
William De Morgan, vase.
Earthenware painted with
lustre. Britain, 1888–98. Made at
the De Morgan Works, Fulham.
V&A: C.417-1919

16 OPPOSITE
W.A.S. Benson, fire screen.
Copper and brass. Britain, 1884.
Made by W.A.S. Benson & Co.
Ltd, London.
V&A: M.37-1972

17 OPPOSITE (RIGHT)
Arthur Dixon, lamp. Brass.
Britain, c.1893. Made by the
Birmingham Guild of
Handicraft.
V&A: Circ.277-1961

18 BELOW
Archibald Knox, tea and coffee
service. Silver, ivory, lapis lazuli.
Britain, 1902–3. Made by W.H.
Haseler for Liberty & Co.
V&A: M.8-2004

19 OPPOSITE
Henry Wilson, chalice. Silver,
partly gilt, ivory and enamel.
Britain, c.1898.
St Bartholomew's Church, Brighton

domestic objects in copper and brass (PLATE 16). These were made using mechanical batch production at his Metal Works in London, which by 1895 employed several hundred people. In 1890 Arthur Dixon founded the Birmingham Guild of Handicraft, a cooperative venture with the aim of producing simple, predominantly hand-produced, domestic metalwares under the motto 'By Hammer and Hand' (PLATE 17). In the same city Liberty & Co. had silver and pewter objects and jewellery made for the London market to designs by Archibald Knox and others. The service illustrated was among the most ambitious and accomplished of Knox's designs, made to the highest standards of craftsmanship by W.H. Haseler Ltd, one of the most important and progressive silver and jewellery manufacturers of the early twentieth century (PLATE 18). Likewise, many individuals, including Henry Wilson, ran small independent workshops. Newly built and refurbished churches were an important source of commissions for many Arts and Crafts designers and makers like Wilson (PLATE 19).

The Arts and Crafts Movement developed in major cities such as London, Birmingham, Liverpool, Manchester, Glasgow and Dublin. Each of these cities had an identifiable and distinctive approach to Arts and Crafts, which was principally organized in Britain on a regional, rather than a national level. Art schools played an important role in establishing the identity of the movement in cities. Through practical classes they encouraged the development of many crafts, including jewellery, calligraphy and illumination (PLATE 20). Glasgow School of Art was particularly noted for its innovative embroidery, taught from 1894 in classes run by Jessie Newbery (PLATE 21), and for the work of one of its students, Charles Rennie Mackintosh. Mackintosh went on to be an architect and designer whose work was highly regarded and influential in Europe. He designed several buildings and interiors, complete with furnishings (PLATE 22), which exemplified the concept of the *Gesamtkunstwerk*. Phoebe Anna Traquair, who lived and worked in Edinburgh, was not affiliated to a single institution. Her highly original work, in enamel, jewellery, book illumination, mural decoration and embroidery, was inspired by a mixture of Italian Renaissance art, classical legends and Celtic sources. The subject matter for the set of four embroidered panels illustrated is based on Walter Pater's *Imaginary Portraits*, a book of historical fantasies first published in 1887 (PLATE 23).

20
Louise Lessore Powell, 'Gloria in Altissimis Deo', calligraphic manuscript. Text from the Gospel according to St Luke, chapter 2, verse 14. Written on vellum in gold on an illuminated floral ground. Britain, 1905.
V&A: L.4396-1959

LET·GLASGOW·FLOVRISH

21 LEFT
Ann Macbeth and Jessie
Newbery, banner for the Royal
Society for the Advancement
of Science. Appliqué linen and
silks. Britain, 1901.
British Association for the
Advancement of Science

22 OPPOSITE
Charles Rennie Mackintosh,
writing desk. Ebonized
mahogany inlaid with mother of
pearl, coloured glass and leaded
glass panel. Britain, 1904.
Designed for Walter Blackie for
Hill House, Helensburgh.
National Trust for Scotland and
Glasgow Museums and Art Gallery

23 PAGES 30 & 31
Phoebe Anna Traquair,
The Progress of a Soul, four
embroidered panels for a
screen. Linen embroidered
with silks and gold thread.
Britain, 1895–1902.
National Gallery of Scotland

24
Ernest Gimson and Alfred
Powell, cupboard painted with
Cotswold scenes. Oak. Britain,
c.1913. For the artist William
Rothenstein.
Private collection

Workshops and communities

For many, the pull of the countryside, and the simple, healthy and (for a few) cultured life that it promised was strong. This was reflected in the types of furnishings produced for and by those who made the move towards a new life (PLATE 24). C.R. Ashbee, who founded the Guild of Handicraft in the East End of London (1888), was perhaps the most famous example of an Arts and Crafts designer to advocate a move to the countryside. In 1902 he encouraged the staff and families of his London workshops to move to the village of Chipping Campden in the Cotswolds, Gloucestershire, in pursuit of a simpler way of life and to follow his belief that 'the proper place for the Arts and Crafts is in the country'.[5] The Guild of Handicraft was to become an influential model for the establishment of other Arts and Crafts guilds and workshops, particularly in Europe and America. Ashbee wrote of the frustrations of work and life in both town and country,[6] but held a strong belief in the dignity of labour associated with workshop production and the cooperative spirit it induces.[7] The Guild's most successful work was its jewellery and beaten silver, usually made to Ashbee's designs (PLATES 25, 26).

In addition to the Cotswolds, Arts and Crafts workshops and communities were established in several other rural locations, including the Lake District, Surrey and Cornwall, the last notable for the manufacture

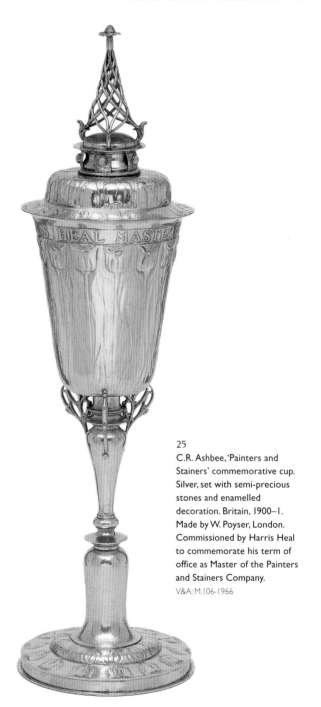

25
C.R. Ashbee, 'Painters and Stainers' commemorative cup. Silver, set with semi-precious stones and enamelled decoration. Britain, 1900–1. Made by W. Poyser, London. Commissioned by Harris Heal to commemorate his term of office as Master of the Painters and Stainers Company.
V&A: M.106-1966

of repoussé copper work, a technique introduced to the area by John Pearson, a former member of the Guild of Handicraft (PLATE 27). Images of the sea and coastal traditions were just as important as rural farming life, particularly to exponents working in the South-West. These were vividly depicted in the paintings of the Newlyn School, adherents of which had formed an artists' colony in Newlyn, Cornwall, in the early 1880s (PLATE 28).

The Haslemere Peasant Industries was a community of artist-craftsmen set up in Surrey in 1894 in an effort to obtain 'the double pleasure of lovely surroundings and happy work'.[8] Various workshops produced

26 OPPOSITE (LEFT)
C.R. Ashbee, pendant and
necklace. Silver and gold, set
with blister pearls, diamond
sparks, demantoid garnet,
pearls. Britain, 1901–2. Made
by the Guild of Handicraft.
V&A: M.23-1965

27 OPPOSITE (ABOVE)
John Pearson, charger. Copper.
Britain, c.1895.
Albert Dawson Collection

28 ABOVE
Stanhope Alexander Forbes,
A Fish Sale on a Cornish Beach.
Oil on canvas. Britain, 1885.
Plymouth City Museum and
Art Gallery

29 ABOVE
Godfrey Blount, *The Spies*,
hanging. Appliqué panel of
hand-woven linen on linen
embroidered with silks. Britain,
c.1900. Embroidered by the
Haslemere Peasant Industries.
V&A: T.218-1953

30 OPPOSITE
Ernest Barnsley, wardrobe.
Oak. Britain, 1902. Made at
Daneway House Workshops,
Gloucestershire, for the
designer's home, Upper Dorvel
House, Sapperton.
V&A: W.39-1977

31
Ernest Gimson, cabinet on
stand. Veneer of macassar
ebony and satinwood, drawers
in cedar veneered with
satinwood. Britain, 1902–5.
Private collection.

ironwork, pottery, woodwork, fresco painting, hand-press printing, bookbinding, plasterwork, carving and textiles. From 1896 their plain fabrics were used in so-called 'Peasant tapestries' made by the Peasant Arts Society, which was founded by Godfrey Blount and trained local women in weaving and embroidery techniques (PLATE 29).

After training as architects and experimenting with the London cabinet-making enterprise Kenton & Co., Ernest Gimson and brothers Sidney and Ernest Barnsley moved to the Cotswolds to make furniture following local traditions and workshop practices. Many of their pieces were based on rural forms such as ladderback chairs and oak dressers or wardrobes (PLATE 30), while others drew on eighteenth-century techniques such as inlay and marquetry. Some of the furniture was simple and plain, other pieces complex and sophisticated, more suitable for the London market (PLATE 31).

Not all Arts and Crafts guilds and workshops were based in the countryside, however. The embroiderer Mary Newill, who had attended and later taught at Birmingham School of Art, was a member of the Bromsgrove Guild of Applied Arts, which had various workshops in Rugby, Bromsgrove and Birmingham, each run by a guild member. Newill ran the guild's embroidery workshops in Birmingham, and in a sense her life and work straddled city (where it was made) and country (in imagery and idealism) (PLATE 32).

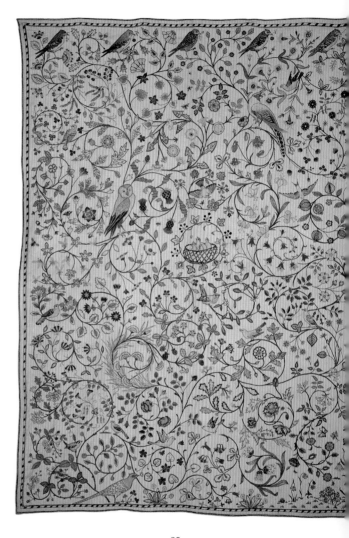

32
Mary Newill, *The Owls*, embroidered hanging. Wool on linen. Britain, c. 1905–8.
Birmingham Institute of Art and Design, University of Central England

33 BELOW
Haydee Ward-Higgs at home in
Bayswater, London, with desk
and chair designed by C.F.A.
Voysey, c.1908–10.
Cheltenham Art Gallery and Museum

34 OPPOSITE
Sidney Barnsley's living room
in Pinbury, Gloucestershire.
Photograph taken by his brother,
Herbert, in the late 1890s.
Cheltenham Art Gallery and Museum

The Arts and Crafts home

Arts and Crafts homes in Britain could range
from the simplest country cottage to a grand
London mansion house. They combined
both the conventional and the radical, often
mixing new and old furnishings but also
including modern features such as electric
lighting, and could be designed and
decorated in either 'Simplicity or Splendour'.[9]

The urban home of William Ward-Higgs, a
successful solicitor in the City of London,
and his wife Haydee reflected their advanced
artistic tastes. In 1896 they commissioned
the architect C.F.A. Voysey to furnish the
house that they had leased in the London
suburb of Bayswater. A number of new pieces
of furniture were made to Voysey's designs,
including a matching desk and armchair for
Haydee Ward-Higgs (PLATE 33) and a second
desk with a pierced copper frieze (see
contents page). These were predominantly
simply designed, architectural pieces, made
of plain oak with minimal decoration.
Whereas Voysey often took a purist approach
to his interiors, carefully designing every
detail, the rooms in this house were
eclectically furnished, reflecting a typically
sophisticated, intellectual, urban style of
Arts and Crafts home that was comfortable
and practical, and mixed new and old
furnishings. An early example of this
approach to furnishing and decorating was
established in the 1890s at Standen in
Sussex, designed by Philip Webb for the

London solicitor James Beale and his family, and by the printer Emery Walker at his home in Hammersmith, London.

A simpler life and home was preferred by those Arts and Crafts designers and makers who lived and worked in the countryside. Often they lovingly restored and adapted historic, vernacular buildings for their own use, supporting the revival of traditional crafts such as decorative plasterwork. Sidney Barnsley moved to the Cotswolds in Gloucestershire in 1893. He lived for a time in a cottage converted from the farm outbuildings in the grounds of Pinbury Park, an Elizabethan house that had been leased by his brother Ernest and his family. The simple furnishings in Sidney Barnsley's cottage included a large bow-fronted oak dresser designed and made by him in about 1898. This room also had a traditional inglenook arrangement, a feature often found in Arts and Crafts rooms where the fireplace and built-in furniture became the focus and, literally, warm heart of the home (PLATE 34). The simplicity of such a room, with its stone floor and plastered walls, reflected not only the simple, hard-working outdoor country life that its owner aspired to, but was also practical. Both cleanliness and healthiness were keen concerns at the end of the nineteenth and early twentieth century, and are reflected in the lightness and plainness of the decoration and furnishings of many Arts and Crafts homes.

The role and status of larger country houses changed in the late nineteenth century, as railways made it easier for industrialists and businessmen to own summer homes in the countryside within commuting distance of the city. One exceptional example of an Arts and Crafts country house of this status is Blackwell, which overlooks Windermere in the Lake District. Blackwell was the country retreat of Sir Edward Holt, prosperous owner of a Manchester brewery, designed for him by M.H. Baillie Scott in 1898. The house is a synthesis of architecture, interiors, garden and landscape. The architect has exploited the picturesque location, and the decorative

35
M.H. Baillie Scott, the White
Drawing Room at Blackwell,
Bowness-on-Windermere.
Designed for Sir Edward Holt.
1898–1900.

detailing that runs through the house – in the stained-glass windows, plasterwork, carved wood and stone, mosaic floors, tiles and stencilling, for example – refers back to the landscape and to the Holt family, whose crest incorporated the rowan leaves and berries of the mountain ash, a tree also common to the Lake District. The three main reception rooms on the ground floor are linked, in a remarkable arrangement, by a long corridor that leads progressively from the dark wood of the main hall and dining room to the light-filled, white drawing room, with its painted and carved inglenook and feeling of modern elegance (PLATE 35).

Baillie Scott, perhaps more than any other British Arts and Crafts architect, wrote extensively on his philosophy of the home and interior. Although he did not design all the furnishings at Blackwell, he applied an intensity of vision and intent to both the single items of furniture he designed for commercial production and to every detail and aspect of a complete home or interior, however simple or splendid (PLATES 36, 37).

36 OPPOSITE
M.H. Baillie Scott, 'Manxman' piano. Ebonized mahogany, carved wood, pewter, mother of pearl, marquetry of stained woods, silver plated handles and hinges. Britain, designed in 1896, made in 1902–3. Movement made by John Broadwood & Sons Ltd., London, case possibly by Broadwood, the Guild of Handicraft or the Pyghtle Works.
V&A: W.15-1976

37 ABOVE
M.H. Baillie Scott, window. Leaded stained glass. Britain, 1902. For the music room of Dr R. K., Mannheim, Germany.
Museum Kunstlerkölonie, Darmstadt.

AMERICA

From east to west: Arts and Crafts in America

The Arts and Crafts Movement in America was bolder and more commercially aware than in Britain, but it also maintained a strong focus on craftsmanship and the essential ideals that underpinned the movement. Exchanges of ideas between Britain and America were frequent and visible. The writings and work of Ruskin, Morris, Ashbee, Baillie Scott and others were well known in America, and were a significant influence on how the movement shaped itself there. However, the Arts and Crafts Movement in America developed not only from international influences but also became an opportunity to find a particularly American style and expression that reflected the confidence and prosperity of this relatively newly established nation. The culture and crafts of Native American Indians was of particular interest. Traditional Indian crafts were featured in Arts and Crafts publications and homes, and were used as a source of inspiration for new work (PLATE 38) while powerful images recorded aspects of the lives of the native nations (PLATE 39).

38 OPPOSITE
Paulding Farnham, bowl. Silver, copper and turquoise. America, c.1900. Made by Tiffany & Co.
High Museum of Art, Atlanta

39 ABOVE
Edward Sheriff Curtis, *Cañon de Chelly – Navaho*. Warm-toned silver print on matte paper. America, 1904.
Collection of Christopher Cardozo

40
Byrdcliffe Colony, cabinet.
Poplar, brass, with carved and
polychromed panel decoration.
America, 1904. Panel with tulip
poplar seeds and leaves
designed by Edna Walker.
The Huntington Library, Art
Collections and Botanical Gardens

Many Arts and Crafts societies and several experimental communities were established in America, modelled on British prototypes. Notable among these were the Byrdcliffe Colony, in Woodstock, New York, established by Ralph Whitehead (PLATE 40), Elbert Hubbard's Roycroft Shops in East Aurora, New York (PLATE 41), and Gustav Stickley's Craftsman Farms, in New Jersey. An entrepreneur and furniture manufacturer with Arts and Crafts vision, Stickley founded the Craftsman Workshops in Syracuse, New York, for the production of metalwork, furniture (PLATE 42) and textiles, and also designed whole houses and interiors (SEE PLATES 50–52). The Craftsman Farms project represented Stickley's vision, not fully realized, to create a model farm with a cooperative community of homeowners, which included educational facilities, but where in the event Stickley made a home for himself and his family. The production of art pottery was also closely associated with the early development of the movement in America. Through this medium connections between craft and industry were established, and it was a field in which ideas about social reform could be explored through the provision of opportunities for women and immigrant communities (PLATES 43, 44).

41
Karl Kipp, jardinière or fern
dish. Hammered copper and
German silver. America,
1910–11. Made by the Roycroft
Copper Shop.
Private collection

42 OPPOSITE
Harvey Ellis for Gustav Stickley,
drop-front desk. Oak inlaid
with pewter, copper and tinted
woods. America, c.1903–4.
Made at the Craftsman
Workshops, Syracuse, New York.
Private collection

43 RIGHT (ABOVE)
William J. Dodd, 'Teco' pottery
vase. Earthenware with green
glaze. Made by the Gates
Potteries. America, 1906.
Private collection

44 RIGHT
Adelaide Alsop Robineau,
Viking Ship vase. Porcelain.
America, 1905.
Collection of Everson Museum of Art,
Syracuse, New York

45
George Mann Niedecken,
perspective rendering of the
dining room of the Susan
Lawrence Dana house,
Springfield, Illinois. Pencil,
pastels and washes on brown
paper. America, c.1903.
Avery Library, Colombia University,
New York

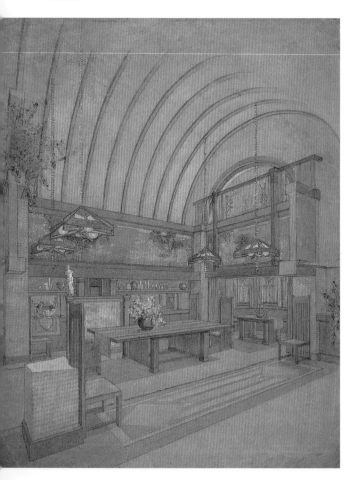

Chicago was at the heartland of American expansion and economic development, and the city provided a fertile ground for the development and patronage of the movement in the Midwest. Progressive architects and designers such as George W. Maher and Frank Lloyd Wright, for example, introduced revolutionary changes in design, opening up interiors, banishing applied ornament and instead integrating features such as stained glass into spaces defined by the design of the furniture (PLATES 45–7).

In California, on the most westerly edge of North America, the natural beauty and inviting climate encouraged a very individual response to Arts and Crafts ideals. Both more independent than and isolated from Arts and Crafts activity in other parts of the country, the Arts and Crafts of California were inspired by the landscape, with architecture shaped by the climate and more relaxed lifestyles. There was a strong feeling of individualism, even at the highest level of bespoke craftsmanship found in the architecture and furnishings of Greene and Greene, California's foremost Arts and Crafts architects (SEE PLATES 53–5). Cities such as San Francisco offered opportunity for the development of new workshops and furnishing styles, most notably achieved by the metalworker Dirk van Erp, and the furniture designed and made by The Furniture Shop (PLATES 48, 49).

46
Frank Lloyd Wright, urn.
Copper. America, c.1903.
One of a pair from the Susan
Lawrence Dana house,
Springfield, Illinois. Made by
James A. Miller, Chicago.
V&A: M.28-1992

47
George Washington Maher,
armchair. Oak, leather. America,
c.1912. From 'Rockledge',
the E.L. King house, Homer,
Minnesota.
The Minneapolis Institute of Arts

48 ABOVE
Dirk van Erp, table lamp.
Copper and mica.
America, c.1910.
Private collection

49 OPPOSITE
Lucia K. Mathews, screen.
Painted and gilt wood.
America, c.1910–15. Made
by the Furniture Shop.
Oakland Museum of California

50 ABOVE
A Craftsman house. *The Craftsman*, December 1904.

51 OPPOSITE
Living room of a Craftsman house. *The Craftsman*, October 1905.

The Craftsman house

Gustav Stickley was one of the most influential American Arts and Crafts designers and manufacturers who, through publishing, marketing, exhibitions and commercial production, defined, for a very wide section of the public, what an Arts and Crafts home in America should look like. From 1901 to 1916 Stickley published *The Craftsman* magazine, the most widely read publication of the American Arts and Crafts Movement. From 1904 the magazine regularly featured homes and interiors designed in the Craftsman style. These modest, sturdy homes, often on one floor, ideally built of local wood and stone, were aimed at a middle-class market. They were reasonably priced and were designed to be suitable for urban, suburban or rural locations and were characterized by open plan living areas, built-in furniture and harmonious colour schemes (PLATES 50, 51). The examples illustrated in the magazine also show Stickley's own, predominantly oak furniture made at the Craftsman Workshops (PLATE 52). The style was frequently featured in other architectural and home decoration

52
Gustav Stickley, book cabinet.
Oak, glass, copper hardware.
America, 1902. Made at the
Craftsman Workshops,
Syracuse, New York.
Private collection

journals, and in newspapers, ensuring that it reached a very wide audience.

The Craftsman home was written about and marketed in such a way that it appealed to the concept of the home as the heart of the family, and at the centre of an American way of life. Through Craftsman houses Stickley not only promoted the furniture, textiles and metalwork that he manufactured, he was also selling a lifestyle. These homes were presented as a sanctuary from working life. The American-made oak furniture represented stability and permanence, and to the housewife a Craftsman home was promoted as the place that would keep her husband at home rather than out at the saloon.

Stickley's concept of the American home appears to have been adopted wholeheartedly by people across the country. The total number of houses built from Stickley plans remains unknown, but, according to one study, $10 million worth of homes had been constructed in the Craftsman style by 1915. At the time the cost of a Craftsman home was between $2000 and $6000, and the average income for a middle-class family was between $1000 and $2000 a year.[10] The Craftsman style also became popular for summer and winter resorts and holiday homes, incorporating associations with log cabins and the outdoor lifestyle beginning to be enjoyed by so many in the early twentieth century.

The Greene and Greene House

The development and popularity of the Arts and Crafts bungalow style in architecture was one of the lasting legacies of the movement in America. It was, however, the architects Charles Sumner Greene and Henry Mather Greene who elevated the status of the Californian bungalow to an unsurpassed level of craftsmanship and design, and who were among the most successful at creating, for very wealthy clients, an American home as a totally coordinated living environment or work of art, in line with the European concept of the *Gesamtkunstwerk*.

53
Charles Sumner Greene and
Henry Mather Greene,
David B. Gamble House,
Pasadena. 1907–9.
Greene and Greene Archives,
The Gamble House, University of
Southern California

Of the masterpieces the Greenes designed and built between 1907 and 1909, the David B. Gamble House in Pasadena, a suburb of Los Angeles, is the only example that survives today complete with its original furnishings. The Gamble House was commissioned as the winter home of the heir to the Proctor and Gamble fortune. With its low eaves, in part inspired by Japanese architecture, the house was designed to suit the temperate Californian climate and to offer a certain amount of outdoor living through the provision, for example, of sleeping porches (PLATE 53). The richly coloured and beautifully crafted interiors are notable for the sumptuous use of Californian redwoods in exquisite joinery, the subtle play of light through stained-glass windows and doors, and the unique suites of furniture designed and flawlessly handcrafted specifically for this house. The living room had more individual pieces created specifically for it than any other room in the house, including the rugs, furniture and light fittings (PLATE 54). Many of the other rooms had distinctive pieces of furniture designed and made for them, including this writing desk from the guest bedroom, which has a removable letter box (PLATE 55).

54 OPPOSITE
Charles Sumner Greene and Henry Mather Greene, living room of the David B. Gamble House, Pasadena. 1907–9.

55 BELOW
Charles Sumner Greene and Henry Mather Greene, desk and letter box. Maple, figured maple, oak, ebony, silver. America, 1908.
David B. Gamble House, Pasadena.

56 BELOW
Richard Riemerschmid, table
and chair for a music room.
Stained oak, leather.
Germany, 1898–9. Chair made
by Liberty & Co., table made
by the Vereinigte Werkstätten
für Kunst und Handwerk,
Munich.
V&A: W.1-1990; Circ.859-1956

57 OPPOSITE
Ernst Riegel, goblet. Silver,
gilded silver and uncut opals.
Germany, 1903.
Stadtmuseum, Munich

EUROPE

Germany and Austria

The Arts and Crafts Movement in Europe developed in different ways, influenced by the political and social stability of the region or country, and determined by varying levels of acceptance of Arts and Crafts ideals. Both German and Austrian Arts and Crafts were directly inspired by British precedent, but evolved in quite different but remarkable and influential ways. In Germany new companies, workshops and art schools were established to design and manufacture good quality, everyday goods as a means of boosting local economies, as well as achieving social reform and elevating the status of the applied arts. Here, it was thought that the British model was too anti-industrial in spirit and that it was appropriate to use technology in production as long as the quality of the product was not compromised (PLATES 56–8). Artists' colonies such as the one founded in Darmstadt aimed to promote community living as well as work with existing industries (PLATE 59).

58 OPPOSITE (LEFT)
Henry van de Velde, samovar
or tea urn. Silver, bone.
Germany, c.1906. Made by
Theodor Müller, Weimar.
Hessisches Landesmuseum, Darmstadt

59 OPPOSITE
Joseph Maria Olbrich,
*Darmstadt, Die Ausstellung der
Künstler-kolonie*, poster. Colour
lithograph. Germany, 1901.
Printed by H. Hohmann,
Darmstadt.
V&A: E.404-1982

60 BELOW
Josef Hoffmann, tea and coffee
service. Silver, ebony, natural
fibre. Austria, 1904. Made by the
Wiener Werkstätte.
Private collection

I n Austria the Wiener Werkstätte, influenced
by C.R. Ashbee's Guild of Handicraft,
which its founder, Josef Hoffmann, had
visited in 1902, adopted a very distinctive
and purist approach to Arts and Crafts. Its
products, including silver, furniture, textiles
and dress, reflected the sophisticated
avant-garde mood of the city, and of the
designers and their fashionably elite patrons
(PLATES 60–62). As a great cultural centre at the
forefront of developments in music,
psychology, the natural sciences and the
visual arts (led by the collaboration of artists
like Gustav Klimt and Josef Hoffmann),
Austria produced designs that stood in
marked contrast to its Hungarian neighbours
both stylistically and politically.

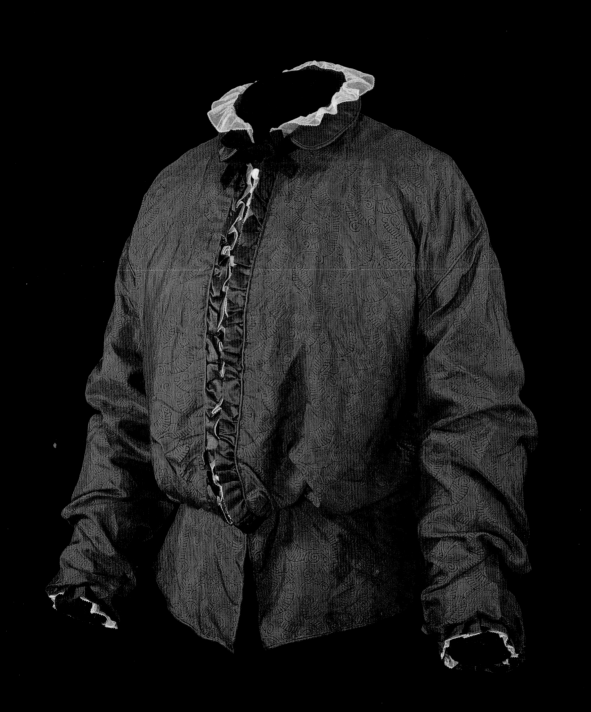

61 OPPOSITE
Eduard Wimmer-Wisgrill (attr.),
blouse. Printed silk; 'Mikado'
pattern designed by Ugo
Zovetti 1910–12, linen, lace,
pearl buttons. Austria, c.1915.
Made by the Wiener Werkstätte.
V&A: T.47-2004

62 RIGHT
Koloman Moser, desk and
integrated armchair. Deal, oak
and mahogany, veneers of thuya
wood, inlaid with satinwood
and brass. Austria, 1903.
Designed for the Hölz
apartment, Vienna. Made by
Caspar Hradzil.
V&A: W.8&a-1982

János Vaszary, *Little Girl with Kitten*, tapestry. Woven wool on cotton. Hungary, 1901. Woven by Sarolta Koválszky at the Némertelemér Workshops.
Museum of Applied Arts, Budapest

József Rippl-Rónai, vase. Glazed earthenware with iridescent glazes. Hungary, 1898–1900.
Art Institute of Chicago

Hungary and Russia

In Central Europe questions of national identity and political independence contributed significantly to the character of the Arts and Crafts Movement. Many parts of Europe were experiencing political and social turmoil at this time. In Hungary, part of the Austro-Hungarian empire, there was a marked contrast between rural areas and the more prosperous and stable Vienna or even Budapest. A rediscovery of peasant and vernacular folk art and architecture inspired the revival of techniques and the development of new work by artist-designers in different media (PLATES 63, 64).

Russia also went through a period of redefining its national identity and its international profile. In the Russian Arts and Crafts Movement this was most clearly expressed in the products of the Abramtsevo and Talashkino workshops (PLATES 65–7). Inspired by the study of traditional crafts and borrowing motifs from the folk art of peasant communities, these workshops evolved a new form of Russian craft and decoration. They were supervised by their wealthy and educated founders, whose intention, nonetheless, was to encourage not only the survival but the development of Russian craft traditions.

67
Princess Maria Tenisheva, box
in the shape of an owl. Silver,
copper, champlevé enamel and
semi-precious stones.
Russia, c. 1904.
Robert and Maurine Rothschild
Family Collection

65 ABOVE
Aleksei Prokofevich Zinoviev
(attr.), hanging. Embroidered
linen. Russian, c. 1900. Made by
the Talashkino artists' colony.
Bankfield Museum, Halifax

66 OPPOSITE
Elena Polenova, wall cupboard.
Painted birch. Russia,
c. 1885–90. Made at the
furniture workshop at the
Abramtsevo artists' colony.
V&A: W.4-2004

68
Lars Kinsarvik, armchair.
Painted wood. Norway, c.1900.
Cecil Higgins Art Gallery,
Bedford, England

Scandinavia

In Norway, Finland, Denmark and Sweden a
period of political and social redefinition
led to more autonomous, independent
constitutions for these countries and
encouraged the rediscovery of national
traditions and styles, which became a vehicle
for the transformation of the decorative arts.
Archaeological discoveries of Viking ships,
the research and publication of folk legends,
the founding of museums of folk crafts and
rural life such as Skansen in Stockholm, and
a new popular interest in traditional dress all
contributed to a celebration of indigenous
life and traditions and the evolution of new
fashionable styles (PLATE 68).

Developments in the rest of Europe were
closely followed by architects and designers
in Scandinavia through journals such as
The Studio and *Deutsche Kunst und Dekoration*.
German publications were particularly
important for disseminating British
developments in architecture and design.
Das englische Haus (1904–5) by Hermann
Muthesius, who was posted to the German
Embassy in London, provided a detailed
analysis of English architecture and gardens
as an expression of society and presented
his belief that the immediate future belonged
to this style of building. Many also travelled
to the UK to see Red House, by that time the
home of the publisher of *The Studio*, Charles
Holme, and other sights such as Liberty's;
and a few had the opportunity to meet

69
Frida Hansen, *Danaid's Jar*,
tapestry. Wool. Norway,
1914. Designed and woven
by Frida Hansen.
Private Collection

70 BELOW
Alfred William Finch, pitcher.
Glazed earthenware. Finland,
1897–1902. Made by the Iris
Workshops, Porvoo.
The Wolfsonian – Florida International
University, Miami Beach, Florida. The
Mitchell Wolfson Jr. Collection

71 OPPOSITE
Armas Lindgren, dining room
cabinet. Oak. Finland, 1904.
Made by the School of Finland's
General Handicraft Society.
Finnish Design Museum, Helsinki

William Morris and Walter Crane. British Arts and Crafts goods were often exhibited internationally and available in fashionable shops, including Sub Rosa in Stockholm as well as, for example, outlets in Christiana (Oslo), Copenhagen, Paris, Berlin, Frankfurt am Main, and Zurich.

These models of tradition and innovation provided the framework from which new and distinctive work was created in Scandinavia. Norwegian textile artists such as Gerhard Munthe (SEE PLATE 10) and Frida Hansen (PLATE 69) incorporated traditional weaving techniques and colours in rhythmical compositions that borrowed imagery and subject matter from folk tales and classical legends. Munthe was an artist who designed and worked in different media, while Hansen was a weaver and ran her own studio. Both achieved international recognition and success at exhibitions.

Finland was also well represented in international exhibitions, and with the revival of Finnish handicraft traditions the Arts and Crafts Movement found a strong and distinctive expression through architecture and the design of domestic objects. As in all the Scandinavian countries, Finnish groups, workshops and organizations, such as Louis Sparre's Iris Workshops in Porvoo or the Friends of Finnish Handicrafts, were formed for the production of high quality furniture, textiles and ceramics for everyday use, using traditional methods and design sources (PLATES 70, 71).

In Denmark the output of designers such as Thorvald Bindesbøll – who trained as an architect but was better known for his work in ceramics, furniture, embroidery, books and the graphic arts, and silver (PLATE 72) – can be seen as an exemplar of the new attitude to art, craft and design established by the Arts and Crafts Movement in Scandinavia. In this period it achieved international recognition and helped shape the characteristics of Scandinavian design that persist to this day.

72
Thorvald Bindesbøll, three bowls. Silver, partly gilt. Denmark, 1899. Made by A. Michelsen.
V&A: 1612, 1613, 1614-1900

73
Carl Larsson, *When the Children have Gone to Bed* (from a series published in *Ett Hem*). Watercolour on paper. Sweden, 1894–7.
The National Museum of Fine Arts, Stockholm

Gesamtkunstwerk: the home as a total work of art

Through the homes designed and built in Scandinavia by artists and architects for their own use, an ideal of domesticity was created that celebrated a nation's individuality and demonstrated that the home, as well as life within it, could become a work of art. In 1888 the Swedish artist Carl Larsson and his wife Karin acquired their house Lilla Hyttnäss in the village of Sundborn, which they transformed into a 'total work of art' that also held for them a strong moral significance. The Larssons were widely read and conversant with current international trends in design, and their home shows traces of the influence of Japanese and British art and architecture, for example. However, the Larssons' overriding intention was to build an artistic house that embodied and embellished Swedish (especially local) traditions and to actively collaborate and participate in its creation. Karin Larsson designed and made most of the textiles in the house, for example, while much of the painted decoration was done by Carl.

From 1899 Carl Larsson published a number of books on Lilla Hyttnäss. In the first of these, *Ett hem* (A home), he reproduced a set of twenty-four watercolours, which were intended to portray the Larsson house as an ideal home and present the family's life as a model for a secure, stable and happy lifestyle (PLATE 73). The international recognition that resulted from the success of these books, particularly in Germany, led the Larsson house to become a model for domestic Swedish design. Similar projects that attempted to combine national design consciousness with the sophisticated ideal

of a simple life also emerged in Finland at Hvitträsk, designed and built by the architects Eliel Saarinen, Hermann Gesellius and Armas Lindgren in 1901–3 as a rural retreat for their own use; and in Poland, at the House under the Firs, designed and built by the painter and art critic Stanisław Witkiewicz in 1896–7.

In Germany the ideal of the *Gesamtkunstwerk* reached its fullest expression at the Darmstadt artists' colony, founded in 1899 by Ernst Ludwig, Grand Duke of Hesse. Here, the seven artists who joined the community were invited to create practical and innovative new surroundings for themselves in which to work and live with their families. Each artist designed their own house and all its furnishings down to the smallest utilitarian object (PLATES 74–6). The houses were opened to the public as part of the first exhibition at Darmstadt in 1901 to promote these simple but well-furnished dwellings as new models for living. It was the intention at Darmstadt to make this type of good domestic design available to a wide and more average population, rather than an artistic elite. While this was not altogether achieved through the design of complete homes, the artists did also design a wide range of goods, including glass, for manufacture both locally and nationally.

74
Peter Behrens, set of drinking
glasses. Gilded glass.
Germany, 1902.
Museum Künstlerkolonie, Darmstadt

75 OPPOSITE
Peter Behrens, Behrens Haus, Darmstadt. Photographed in 1901.
Die Ausstellung der Darmstädter Künstlerkolonie 1901, Alexander Koch (ed.), Darmstadt, 1901

76 ABOVE
Peter Behrens, Behrens Haus dining room, Darmstadt.
Deutsche Kunst und Dekoration, 1902.

JAPAN

Mingei: art of the people

The Mingei (folk crafts) movement in Japan, which flourished in the period 1926–45, was the last significant manifestation of the Arts and Crafts Movement. It was a radical, modern, progressive movement, led by an urban intellectual elite. It aimed to preserve and revitalize rural folk crafts, and through them to establish a new aesthetic in modern crafts.

Mingei grew out of the association of the theorist and writer Yanagi Sōetsu[11] with the potters Hamada Shōji, Tomimoto Kenkichi, Kawai Kanjirō and the Englishman Bernard Leach, who was born in the Far East and learned the art of pottery in Japan. As Japan became increasingly westernized from the 1860s, and experienced the effects of the growth of industry, this group of makers and thinkers developed an ideology for the revival and reform of traditional crafts through a new appreciation of the vernacular and of everyday objects – the art of the people. They absorbed the ideas of William Morris and John Ruskin, which had first been translated into Japanese in the 1880s and were widely disseminated by 1920. They were also aware of, and inspired by, other European Arts and Crafts activities, such as Skansen, the open-air museum in Stockholm, and the work of artists, designers and craftsman in Britain, Austria and Germany.

Spurred on by his research and documentation of Mokujiki sculptures in remote Japanese villages (PLATE 77), Yanagi discovered and collected folk crafts from every region of Japan (PLATES 78–9), as well as parts of Taiwan and Korea (SEE PLATE 12). In 1936 he founded the Japan Folk Crafts Museum in Tokyo to house the collection of over 10,000 objects that he had assembled. Designed in the style of a traditional farmhouse, it became the exemplar of Mingei architecture and display, and the central institution of the Mingei movement. After the Second World War fifteen further museums were opened across Japan by Yanagi's friends and followers of the Mingei movement. The museums and their associated organizations helped encourage the revitalization of depressed rural craft industries, while Yanagi's appreciation and theoretical study of such everyday art encouraged a new interest in the vernacular and in traditional folk crafts, which remains current in Japan today.

79 OPPOSITE
Spouted bowl (*katakuchi*),
Wajima ware. Lacquered wood.
Japan, 18th century.
Montgomery Collection

80 ABOVE
Hamada Shōji, dish. Stoneware
with *tenmoku* glaze, rice husk
ash glaze and finger-wiped
decoration. Japan, 1944.
Ōhara Museum of Art, Kurashiki, Japan

A new generation

Seven artist-craftsmen played a crucial role
in the development of the Mingei movement.
They were the four potters Hamada, Leach ,
Kawai and Tomimoto (SEE PLATE 12), the textile
artist Serizawa Keisuke, the lacquerer and
woodworker Kuroda Tatsuaki, and the
printmaker Munakata Shikō (PLATES 80–84).
This new generation of named, rather than
anonymous, craft makers in Japan engaged
in both the intellectual and creative pursuits
of the Mingei movement. They debated the
concept of individualism and the place of the
artist-craftsman, and felt a responsibility
towards helping reverse the decline of rural
craft production. The works they made were
concrete expressions of how craft traditions
could continue and develop, and are vital
constituents of what the Mingei movement
stood for.

Two of these makers, Hamada and Leach,
were particularly influential outside Japan.
In a sense they brought the Arts and Crafts
Movement, and subsequent ideas about the
nature of craft work, full circle. In Britain,
the country in which the Arts and Crafts
Movement originated, Hamada and Leach
later became foremost in establishing a new
approach to craft and the individual that
profoundly affected the direction of the craft
movement in Britain, America, Europe and
Japan in the twentieth century.

81
Serizawa Keisuke, six-fold
screen, with illustrated map of
Okinawa. Stencil-dyed silk.
Japan, 1940.
V&A: FE.21-1985

82
Kuroda Tatsuaki, lidded box.
Wood with all-over mother-of-
pearl decoration and red
lacquer. Japan, 1927.
Kagizen Yoshifusa

83 ABOVE
Munakata Shikō, *Shaka Jūdai Deshi* (Ten Great Followers of Shaka), twelve woodcuts. Ink on paper. Japan, 1939.
Ōhara Museum of Art, Kurashiki, Japan

84 OPPOSITE
Bernard Leach, 'Leaping Fish', vase. Stoneware with white glaze painted in iron-brown. Britain, 1931. Made at the Leach Pottery, St Ives.
V&A: Circ.144-1931

Homes for the middle classes

The concept of the home as the environment in which the ideas and philosophies of the Mingei movement could become relevant to contemporary life was central to the way the Arts and Crafts Movement manifested itself in Japan. In 1928 Yanagi and his Mingei colleagues designed the Folk Crafts Pavilion (Mingeikan, later called the Mikunisō) at the Exhibition for the Promotion of Domestic Products in Commemoration of the Enthronement of the Emperor, held in Ueno, Tokyo. It had a series of model rooms that were intended to create a new and modern style of everyday living for the middle classes. They presented a hybrid mix of both Japanese and Western ideas, combining traditional folk crafts with pieces by contemporary Mingei makers, such as the western-style dining room table and chairs by Kuroda (PLATE 85).

Artist-craftsmen such as Leach, Tomimoto, Hamada and Kawai lived in homes that they designed and created as expressions of a very particular aesthetic and intellectual artistic life. The potter Kawai Kanjirō designed and built his own house in the Gojōzaka ceramics district of Kyoto, after his home was destroyed in a typhoon in 1934. It was built in 1937 by a team of skilled craftsmen under the direction

85
Mikunisō, view through dining
room towards master's room.
Asahi Beer Ōyamazaki Villa Museum
of Art

of his brother, a master carpenter, using traditional building methods. From the street the house was intended to merge with and complement the neighbourhood, as Kawai viewed his house not only as his home but also as part of the community in which he lived.

The interior spaces were designed with both respect for tradition and the needs of a contemporary lifestyle, and the house is furnished with Japanese, Korean and western-style furniture, including stools for visitors from overseas not used to sitting close to the floor (PLATE 86). Some of the furniture in the house was designed by Kawai himself and made by local craftsmen, and his friends and associates, including Yanagi, Hamada and Munakata, gifted other pieces. The house was also a showcase for Kawai's own work, which he made in the studio and fired in the kilns at the back of the property. Life in the house was democratic, and it was often filled with so many visitors that meals had to be served in more than one sitting. Through the interpretation and adaptation of vernacular architecture and traditional ways of living, and by combining historical folk crafts with contemporary pieces, Kawai achieved through his lifestyle the aesthetic of a sophisticated, modern, urban space that embodied the spirit of the Mingei movement and emphasized the significance of the home as an expression of the Arts and Crafts ideal.

86
Kawai Kanjirō's house, Kyoto,
main hall.

NOTES

1 Walter Crane, *Ideals in Art* (London, 1905), p.27.

2 A.H. Mackmurdo, 'History of the Arts and Crafts Movement' (unpublished manuscript, William Morris Gallery, Walthamstow), quoted in Linda Parry, *Textiles of the Arts and Crafts Movement* (London, 1988), p.15.

3 Walter Crane, op. cit., p.22.

4 Quoted in Gillian Naylor, *The Arts and Crafts Movement: A Study of its Sources, Ideals and Influence on Design Theory* (London, 1971), p.148.

5 C.R. Ashbee, *Craftsmanship in Competitive Industry* (London and Chipping Campden, 1908), p.11.

6 C.R. Ashbee, op.cit.

7 See C.R. Ashbee, 'Decorative Art from a Workshop Point of View'. A paper read to the Edinburgh Art Congress, 1889, reprinted in *A Few Chapters in Workshop Reconstruction and Citizenship* (London, 1894), pp.39–48.

8 Quoted in Linda Parry, *Textiles of the Arts and Crafts Movement* (London, 1988), p.127.

9 Walter Crane, 1911, quoted in Mary Greensted, *Simplicity or Splendour. Arts and Crafts Living: Objects from the Cheltenham Collections* (London, 1999), p.9.

10 Eileen Boris, *Art and Labor: Ruskin, Morris and the Craftsman Ideal in America* (Philadelphia, 1986), pp.75–7.

11 Japanese names are all given in Japanese order; that is family name followed by given name.

PICTURE CREDITS

Half title, plate 57 Stadtmuseum Munich © Photo: Wolfgang Pulfer

Plates 3, 32 Birmingham Museum and Art Gallery

Plates 5, 46 © ARS, NY and DACS, London 2004

Plates 6, 41, 42, 43, 52 Private collection © A. J. Photographics Design

Plates 7, 37, 74, 75, 76 Städtische Kunstsammlung Darmstadt/Museum Künstlerkolonie

Plates 9, 60 Asenbaum Fine Arts Ltd

Plate 10 Museum für Kunst und Gewerbe Hamburg

Plate 11 National Museum of Modern Art, Tokyo © Ryu Kaido

Plate 12 © Copyright The British Museum

Plates 14 The National Gallery of Scotland © The Estate of John Duncan 2004. All rights reserved, DACS

Plate 19 Photograph by kind permission of St Bartholomew Brighton and the Chapter of Chichester Cathedral

Plates 21, 24, 69 Private Collection © V&A Images

Plate 22 National Trust for Scotland and Glasgow Museums and Art Gallery © Christies Images Ltd 2005

Plate 23 The National Gallery of Scotland

Plate 27 Albert Dawson Collection

Plate 28 Plymouth City Museum and Art Gallery © Courtesy of the Artist's Estate / www.bridgeman.co.uk

Plate 31 Private collection © Photo Paul Highnam

Plate 35 © Lakeland Arts Trust

Plate 38 High Museum of Art, Atlanta, Georgia. Virginia Carroll Crawford Collection, 1984.170

Plate 39 Collection of Christopher Cardozo – Courtesy of Christopher Cardozo Fine Arts

Plate 40 The Huntington Library, Art Collections and Botanical Gardens, San Marino, California. © Photo Rick Echelmeyer, courtesy of Robert Edwards

Plate 44 Collection of Everson Museum of Art. Museum purchase 16.4.1a-b.

Plate 45 Avery Architectural and Fine Arts Library, Columbia University in the City of New York

Plate 47 The Minneapolis Institute of Arts, The Anne and Hadlai Hall Fund, Gift of Mr. and Mrs. Sheldon Sturgis and Gift of Mr. and Mrs. Henry Hyatt

Plate 48 © Photo Erika K. Marrin

Plate 49 Oakland Museum of California, Gift of Concours d'Antiques, the Art Guild. Photo M. Lee Fatherree

Plate 53 Greene and Greene Archives, The Gamble House, University of Southern California

Plate 54 © Photo Mark Fiennes

Plate 55 Photo: Ognan Borissov

Plates 56, 74, 76 © DACS 2004

Plate 58 Hessisches Landesmuseum Darmstadt. Photo Wolfgang Fuhrmannek

Plate 64 Restricted gift of Mr. and Mrs. Henry Buchbinder and Mr. and Mrs. Robert O. Delaney, 1996.12. Reproduction, The Art Institute of Chicago

Plate 65 Calderdale Council, Libraries, Museums and Arts, Bankfield Museum, Halifax. © Photo: Jerry Hardman Jones

Plate 67 Robert and Maurine Rothschild Family Collection

Plate 68 Trustees, Cecil Higgins Art Gallery, Bedford, England

Plate 70 The Wolfsonian – Florida International University, Miami Beach, Florida, The Mitchell Wolfson Jr. Collection

Plate 73 Photo: The National Museum of Fine Arts, Stockholm

Plate 77 Collection of the Japan Folk Crafts Museum

Plate 79 Courtesy of the Montgomery Collection, Ascona, Switzerland. Photo Robert Buzzini

Plates 80, 83 Ōhara Museum of Art, Kurashiki, Japan

Plate 82 Kagizen Yoshifusa. Photo: National Museum of Modern Art, Kyoto

Plate 84 By permission of David Leach

Plate 85 Asahi Beer Ōyamazaki Villa Museum of Art

Plate 86 Kawai Kanjirō's House

PLACES TO VISIT

Many of the houses described in this book
are open to the public, and their addresses
and contact details are listed here.
The Victoria and Albert Museum has one
of the largest and most comprehensive
public collections of Arts and Crafts, and
many other museums internationally have
important collections. Check local
information for details or see
www.artsandcraftsmuseum.org.uk

BRITAIN

Victoria and Albert Museum
Cromwell Road
London SW7 2RL
UK
Tel: + 44 (0)20 7942 2573
www.vam.ac.uk

Standen
West Hoathly Road
East Grinstead
Sussex RH19 4NE
UK
Tel: + 44 (0)1342 323029
www.nationaltrust.org.uk

Blackwell
The Arts and Crafts House
Bowness on Windermere
Cumbria LA23 3JR
UK
Tel: + 44 (0)15394 46139
www.blackwell.org.uk

AMERICA

Craftsman Farms
2352 Route 10 West at Manor Lane
Parsippany-Troy Hills
New Jersey 07950
USA
Tel: + 1 973 540 1165
www.stickleymuseum.org

Frank Lloyd Wright home and studio
951 Chicago Avenue
Oak Park
Illinois 60302
USA
Tel: + 1 708 848 1976
www.wrightplus.org

David B. Gamble House
4 Westmoreland Place
Pasadena
California 91103
USA
Tel: + 1 626 793 3334
www.gamblehouse.org

EUROPE

Lilla Hytnäss: the home of Carl Larsson
Carl Larssonsväg
12 79015 Sundborn
Sweden
Tel: +46 (0)23 600 53
www.carllarsson.se

Darmstadt Artists' Colony
Museum Künstlerkolonie
Institut Mathildenhöhe
Alexandraweg
D-64287 Darmstadt
Germany
Tel: + 49 (0)6151 1327 78
www.mathildenhoehe.info

Hvitträsk
Hvitträskintie 166
FI-02440 Luoma
Finland
Tel: + 358 9 4050 9630
www.hvittrask.fi

JAPAN

Kawai Kanjirō's House
569 Kanei-cho
Gojōzaka
Higashiyama-ku
Kyoto 605-0875
Japan
Tel: + 81 75 561 3585
www.studiomiu.com/kanjiro

FURTHER READING

Anscombe, Isabelle *Arts and Crafts Style* (Oxford, 1991)

Anscombe, Isabelle and Charlotte Gere *Arts and Crafts in Britain and America* (London, 1978)

Ayres, Dianne, Timothy Hansen, Beth Ann McPherson and Tommy Arthur McPherson II *American Arts and Crafts Textiles* (New York, 2002)

Bosley, Edward R *Greene and Greene* (London, 2000)

Bowman, Lesley Greene *American Arts and Crafts: Virtue in Design* (Los Angeles County Museum of Art, exhib. cat., 1990)

Brandstätter, Christian *Wiener Werkstätte: Design in Vienna 1903–1932* (New York, 2003)

Bröhan-Museum *Now the Light Comes from the North: Art Nouveau in Finland* (Bröhan-Museum, Berlin, exhib. cat., 2002)

Burkhauser, Jude (ed.) *'Glasgow Girls': Women in Art and Design, 1880–1920* (Edinburgh, exhib. cat., 1990)

Callen, Anthea *Angel in the Studio* (London, 1979)

Carruthers, Annette, and Mary Greensted (eds) *Simplicity or Splendour. Arts and Crafts Living: Objects from the Cheltenham Collections* (Cheltenham and London, 1999)

Cathers, David *Gustav Stickley* (New York, 2003)

Clark, Robert Judson (ed.) *The Arts and Crafts Movement in America 1876–1916* (Princeton, NJ, exhib. cat., 1972)

Cooper, Jeremy *Victorian and Edwardian Furniture and Interiors: From the Gothic Revival to Art Nouveau* (London, 1987)

Crawford, A *C.R. Ashbee: Architect, Designer & Romantic Socialist* (New Haven and London, 1985)

Crawford, Alan *Charles Rennie Mackintosh* (London, 1995)

Crawford, Alan (ed.) *By Hammer and Hand: The Arts and Crafts Movement in Birmingham* (Birmingham, exhib. cat., 1994)

Cumming, Elizabeth, and Wendy Kaplan *The Arts and Crafts Movement* (London, 1991)

Davey, Peter *Arts and Crafts Architecture* (London, 1980)

De Waal, Edmund *Bernard Leach* (London, 1997)

De Waal, Edmund, R. Faulkner et al *Timeless Beauty: Traditional Japanese Art from the Montgomery Collection* (Milan, 2002)

Gordon Bowe, Nicola (ed.) *Art and the National Dream: The Search for Vernacular Expression in Turn of the Century Design* (Dublin, 1993)

Gordon Bowe, Nicola, and Elizabeth Cumming *The Arts and Crafts Movements in Dublin & Edinburgh, 1885–1925* (Dublin, 1998)

Greenhalgh, Paul (ed.) *Art Nouveau 1890–1914* (London, 2000)

Greensted, Mary *The Arts & Crafts Movement in the Cotswolds* (Stroud, 1992)

Haigh, Diane *Baillie Scott: The Artistic House* (London, 1995)

Harrod, Tanya *The Crafts in Britain in the 20th Century* (New Haven and London, 1999)

Hitchmough, Wendy *The Arts and Crafts Home* (London, 2000)

Howard, Jeremy *Art Nouveau: International and National Styles in Europe* (Manchester, 1996)

Kallir, Jane *Viennese Design and the Wiener Werkstätte* (New York, 1986)

Kaplan, Wendy *'The Art that is Life': The Arts and Crafts Movement in America, 1875–1920* (Boston, exhib. cat., 1987)

Kaplan, Wendy et al *Encyclopaedia of Arts and Crafts: The International Arts Movement 1850–1920* (London, 1989)

Kikuchi, Yuko *Japanese Modernisation and Mingei Theory: Cultural Nationalism and Oriental Orientalism* (London, 2004)

Lambourne, Lionel *Utopian Craftsmen: The Arts and Crafts Movement from the Cotswolds to Chicago* (London, 1980)

Larmour, Paul *The Arts and Crafts Movement in Ireland* (Belfast, 1992)

Livingstone, Karen and Linda Parry (eds) *International Arts and Crafts* (London, 2005)

MacCarthy, Fiona *The Simple Life: C. R. Ashbee in the Cotswolds* (London 1981)

Marsh, Jan *Back to the Land: the Pastoral Impulse in Victorian England* (London, 1982)

Muthesius, H *Das englische Haus* (Berlin, 1904–5; abridged English translation of 2nd edition, ed. D. Sharpe, London, 1979)

Naylor, Gillian *The Arts and Crafts Movement: A Study of its Sources, Ideals and Influence on Design Theory* (London, 1971)

Noever, Peter (ed.) *Der Preis der Schönheit. 100 Jahre Wiener Werkstätte* (Vienna, exhib. cat., 2004)

Parry, Linda *Textiles of the Arts and Crafts Movement* (London, 1988)

Parry, Linda (ed.) *William Morris* (Victoria and Albert Museum, exhib. cat., 1996)

Richardson, Margaret *Architects of the Arts and Crafts Movement* (London, 1983)

Salmond, W *Arts and Crafts in Late Imperial Russia: Reviving the Kustar Art Industries 1870–1917* (Cambridge, 1996)

Savage, Peter *Lorimer and the Edinburgh Craft Designers* (Edinburgh, 1980)

Snodin, Michael and Elisabet Stavenow-Hidemark *Carl and Karin Larsson: Creators of the Swedish Style* (London, 1997)

Stansky, Peter *Redesigning the World: William Morris, the 1880s, and the Arts and Crafts* (Princeton, NJ, 1985)

Stickley, Gustav *Craftsman Homes: Architecture and Furnishings of the American Arts and Crafts Movement* (1909; reprinted, New York, 1979)

Trapp, Kenneth *The Arts and Crafts Movement in California: Living the Good Life* (New York, 1993)

Ulmer, Renate *Museum Künstlerkolonie Darmstadt* (Darmstadt, 1990)

Volpe, Todd and Beth Cathers *Treasures of the American Arts and Crafts Movement* (New York, 1988)

Yanagi Sōetsu, adapted by Bernard Leach *The Unknown Craftsman: A Japanese Insight into Beauty* (Tokyo, 1972)

Journals

Architectural Review (Boston, 1891–1921)

The Architectural Review (London, 1896–)

Art et Décoration (Paris, 1897–1938)

The Art Journal (London, 1839–1912)

The Builder (London, 1842–1966)

The Craftsman (New York, 1901–1916)

Dekorative Kunst (Munich, 1897–1929)

Deutsche Kunst und Dekoration (Darmstadt, 1897–1932)

Furniture and Decoration (London 1893–1899)

The Furniture Record (London, 1899–1962)

The Hobby Horse (London, 1883–1893)

Kōgei (Tokyo, 1938–1940)

Kunst und Kunsthandwerk (Vienna, 1898–1928)

Mir Iskusstva (The World of Art; St Petersburg, 1898–1904)

Der Moderne Stil (Stuttgart, 1899–1905)

The Studio (London, 1893–)

INDEX

Page numbers in italic refer to illustration captions found on those pages.